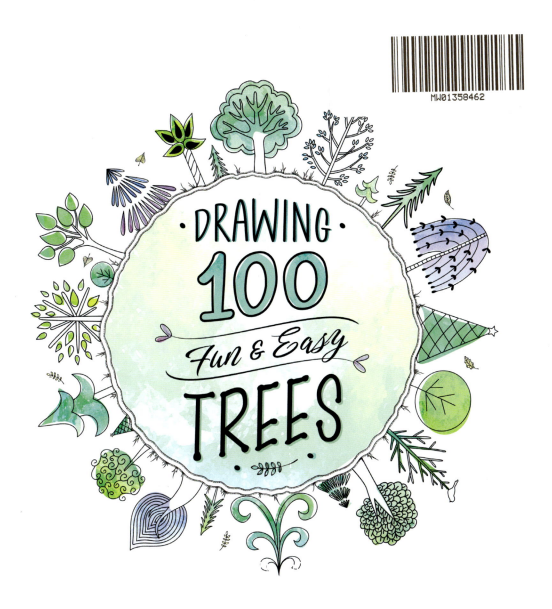

© 2020 Jenny Phillips | goodandbeautiful.com

All rights reserved. No part of this book may be copied or reproduced in any way without written permission from the publisher.

INSTRUCTIONS

MATERIALS NEEDED:

- Standard #2 pencil, sharpened
- Kneaded eraser
- Sketch paper

INSTRUCTIONS:

Depending on the shape of the box around the image you are going to draw (square or rectangle), draw a large square or rectangle on your sketch paper. This will help you scale your image appropriately. Then, draw the images as shown in each step, taking care to press your pencil lightly on the paper as you will need to erase certain elements as you progress through the steps of the project.

TABLE OF CONTENTS

1. Christmas Tree With Lights 1
2. Pointed Tree #1 1
3. Line Tree #1 2
4. Weeping Willow Heart Tree 2
5. Evergreen Tree #1 3
6. Whimsical Palm Tree 3
7. Triangle Tree #1 4
8. Teardrop Tree #1 4
9. Evergreen Tree #2 5
10. Criss-Cross Tree With Star 5
11. Curly Tree #1 6
12. Tree Full of Leaves 6
13. Swirly Tree 7
14. Circle Tree #1 7
15. Blowing Tree 8
16. Chevron Tree #1 8
17. Evergreen Tree #3 9
18. Dotted Tree 9
19. Leafy Tree #1 10
20. Shaggy Tree 10
21. Tree Blowing in the Wind 11
22. Pointed Tree #2 11
23. Tree Trunk 12
24. Evergreen Tree #4 12
25. Tree With Tinsel 13
26. Leaf Tree #1 13
27. Polka Dot Tree #1 14
28. Triangle Plaid Tree 14
29. Snowy Cone Tree 15
30. Triangle Tree #2 15
31. Dotted Maze Tree 16
32. Decorated Stick Tree 16
33. Semicircle Tree 17
34. Lollipop Tree 17
35. Line Tree #2 18
36. Tree With a Bird 18
37. Rainbow Tree 19
38. Dotted Leaf Tree 19
39. Triangle Leaf Tree 20
40. Line Tree #3 20
41. Heart Tree #1 21
42. Lava Tree 21
43. Droopy Tree 22
44. Circle Tree #2 22
45. Square Tile Tree 23
46. Teardrop Tree #2 23
47. Tree With Roots 24
48. Teardrop Tree #3 24
49. Tree With Swirls 25
50. Squiggle Tree 25
51. Bush Tree 26
52. Leaf Tree #2 26
53. Tree With Ribbons 27
54. Multi-Branch Tree 27
55. Swirl Tree 28
56. Squiggly Tree 28
57. Heart Tree #2 29
58. Oval Tree 29

59. Baobab Tree 30	88. Wide Tree 44
60. Triangle Tree #3 30	89. Wooden Board Tree 45
61. Full Tree 31	90. Rainy Tree 45
62. Leafy Tree #2 31	91. Tall Cone Tree 46
63. Eyelash Tree 32	92. Wild Evergreen Tree 46
64. Chevron Tree #2 32	93. Twiggy Tree 47
65. Tree With Many Leaves 33	94. Tall Pointed Tree 47
66. Scalloped Tree 33	95. Big Round Tree 48
67. Geometric Tree 34	96. Leaf Tree #3 48
68. String Tree 34	97. Cactus Tree 49
69. Skinny Tree 35	98. Tree With Berries 49
70. Egg Tree 35	99. Squiggle Tree With a Star 50
71. Bushy Tree 36	100. Flourish Tree 50
72. Large Tree 36	
73. Balloon Tree 37	
74. Snowy Branches Tree 37	
75. Leafy Branches on a Tree 38	
76. Square Tree 38	
77. Twirly Bush Tree 39	
78. Teardrop Tree #4 39	
79. Rosebud Tree 40	
80. Polka Dot Tree #2 40	
81. Evergreen Tree #5 41	
82. Artsy Tree 41	
83. Tornado Tree 42	
84. Curly Tree #2 42	
85. Cone Tree 43	
86. Curl Tree 43	
87. Petal Tree 44	

1 CHRISTMAS TREE WITH LIGHTS

1

2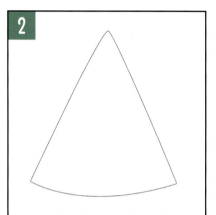

3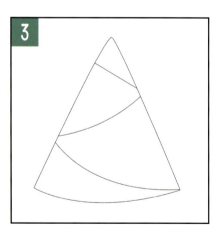

4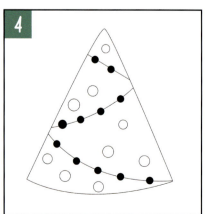

2 POINTED TREE #1

1

2

3

4

3 LINE TREE #1

1

2

3

4 WEEPING WILLOW HEART TREE

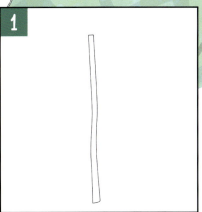

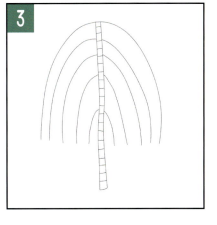

5 EVERGREEN TREE #1

6 WHIMSICAL PALM TREE

7 — TRIANGLE TREE #1

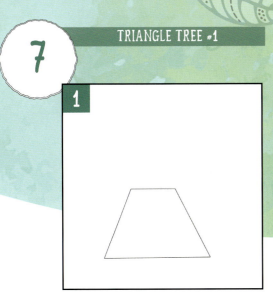

8 — TEARDROP TREE #1

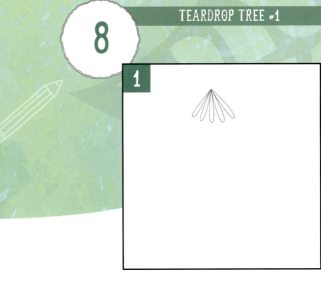

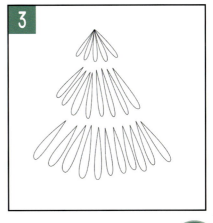
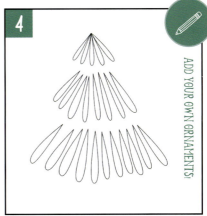

ADD YOUR OWN ORNAMENTS!

9 EVERGREEN TREE #2

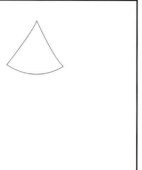

10 CRISS-CROSS TREE WITH STAR

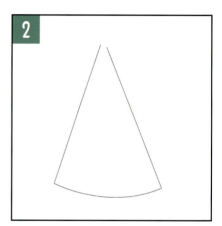

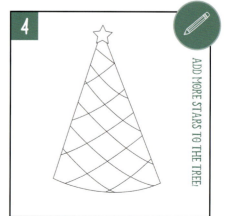

ADD MORE STARS TO THE TREE!

11 — CURLY TREE #1

1

2

3

4

12 — TREE FULL OF LEAVES

1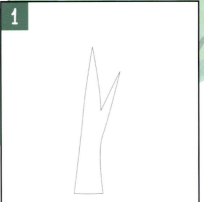

2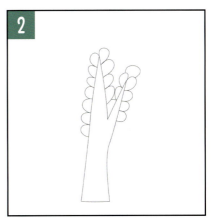

3

4

13 SWIRLY TREE

1
2
3
4

14 CIRCLE TREE #1

1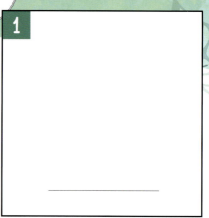
2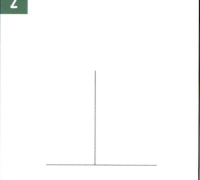
3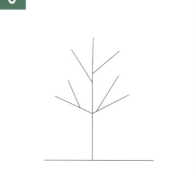
4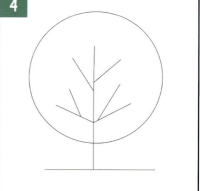

15 BLOWING TREE

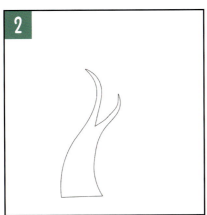

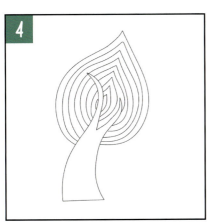

16 CHEVRON TREE #1

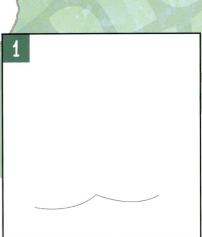

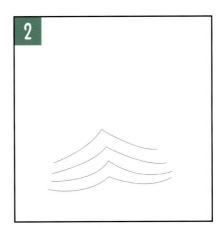

17 EVERGREEN TREE #3

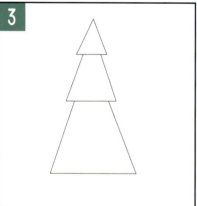

18 DOTTED TREE

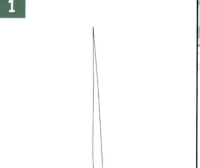

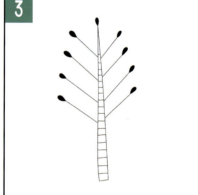
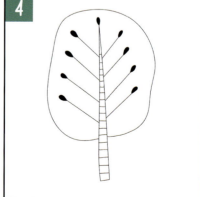

19 — LEAFY TREE #1

20 — SHAGGY TREE

21 TREE BLOWING IN THE WIND

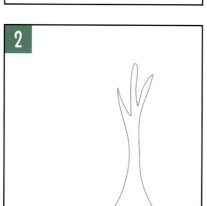

22 POINTED TREE #2

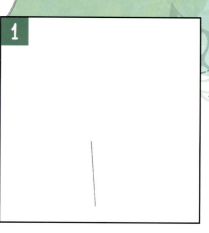

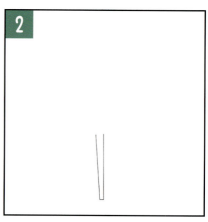

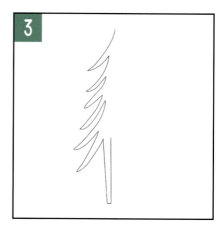

23 TREE TRUNK

1
2
3
4

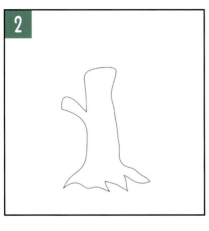
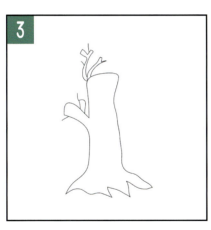

24 EVERGREEN TREE #4

1
2
3
4

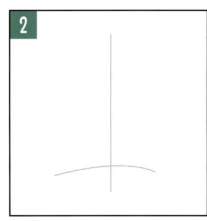
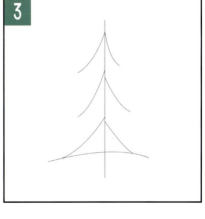

25 TREE WITH TINSEL

26 LEAF TREE #1

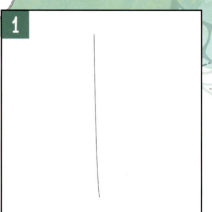
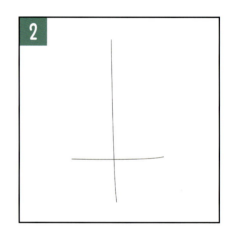
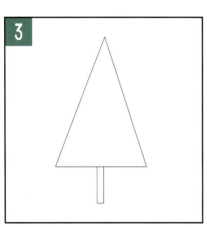
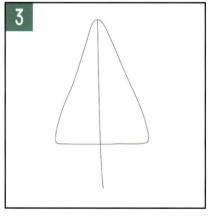

27 POLKA DOT TREE #1

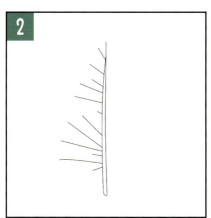

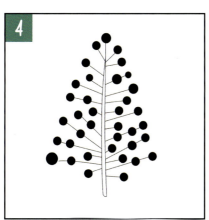

28 TRIANGLE PLAID TREE

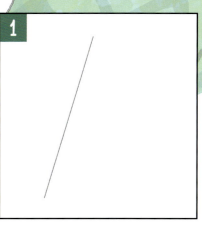

29 SNOWY CONE TREE

1

2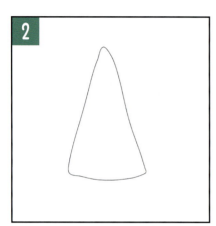

3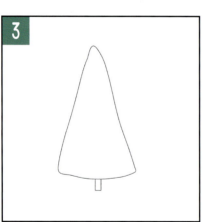

4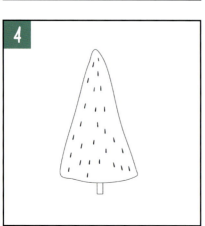

30 TRIANGLE TREE #2

1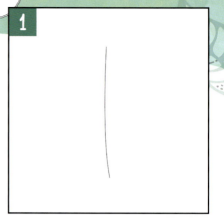

2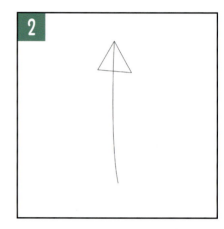

3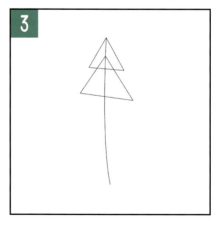

4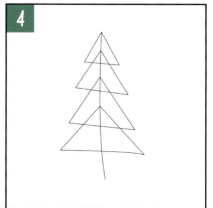

31 — DOTTED MAZE TREE

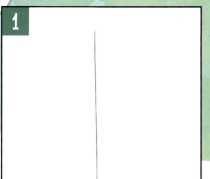
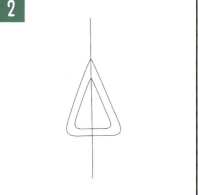

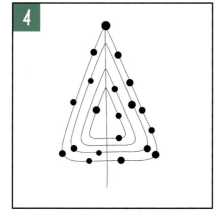

32 — DECORATED STICK TREE

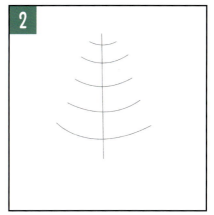
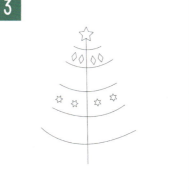

33 SEMICIRCLE TREE

34 LOLLIPOP TREE

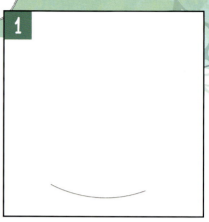
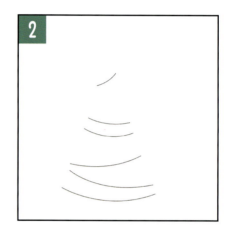
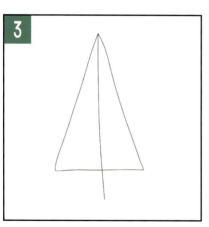

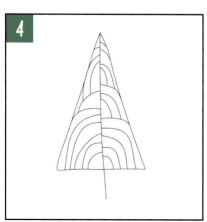

35 LINE TREE #2

36 TREE WITH A BIRD

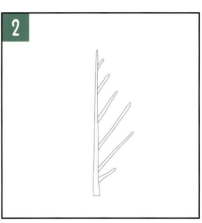

37 RAINBOW TREE

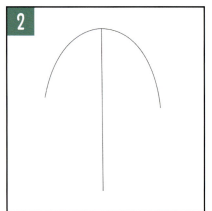
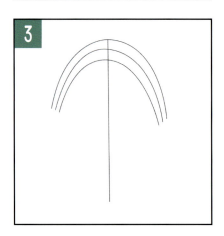
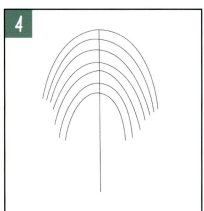

38 DOTTED LEAF TREE

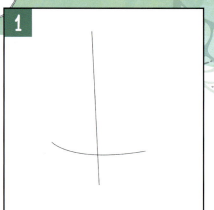
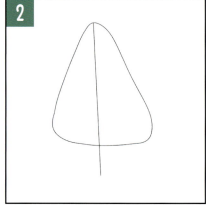
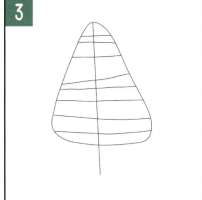
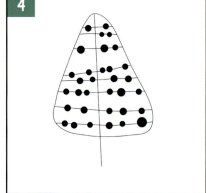

39 TRIANGLE LEAF TREE

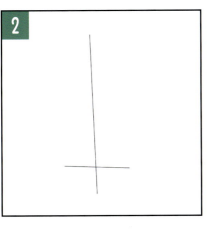

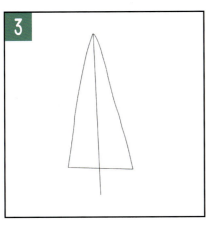

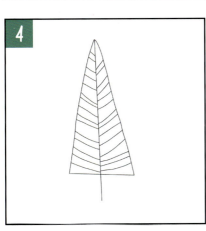

40 LINE TREE #3

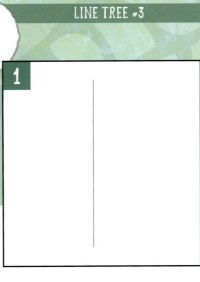

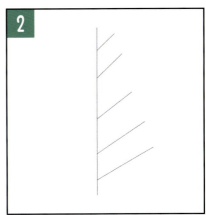

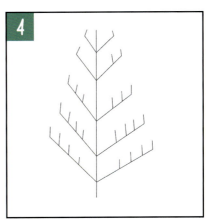

41 HEART TREE #1

42 LAVA TREE

43 DROOPY TREE

44 CIRCLE TREE #2

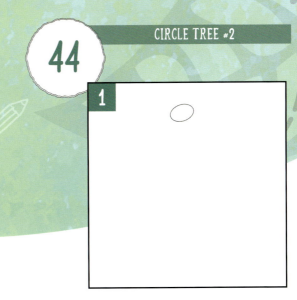

45 SQUARE TILE TREE

1
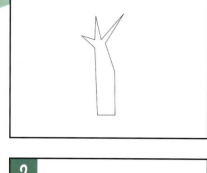

2

3
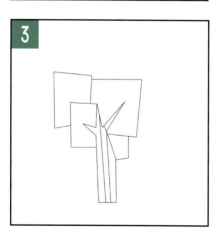

4
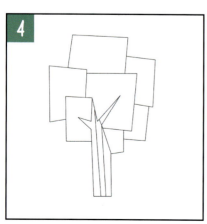

46 TEARDROP TREE #2

1
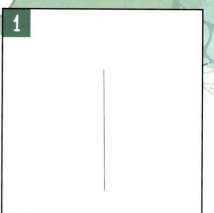

2
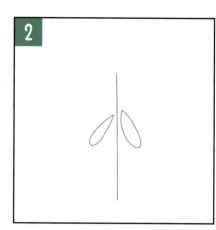

3

4
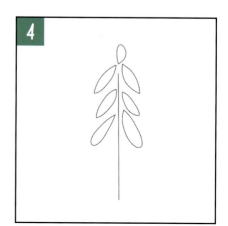

47 TREE WITH ROOTS

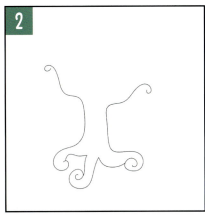
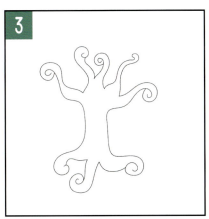

48 TEARDROP TREE #3

49 TREE WITH SWIRLS

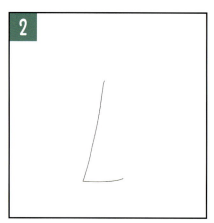

50 SQUIGGLE TREE

51 BUSH TREE

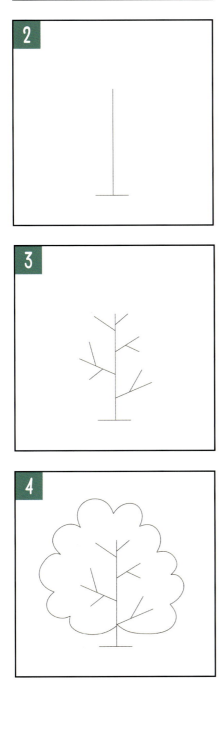

52 LEAF TREE #2

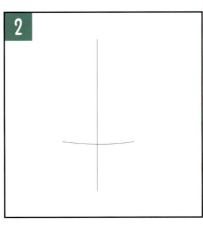
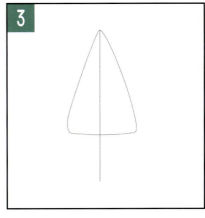
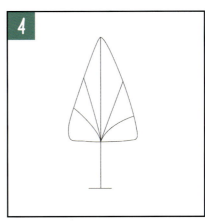

53 TREE WITH RIBBONS

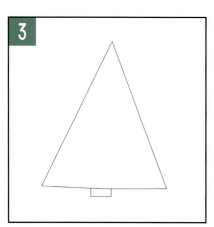

54 MULTI-BRANCH TREE

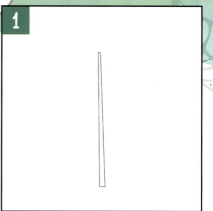
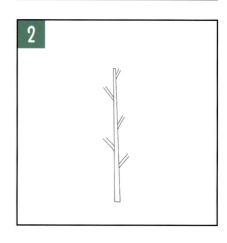

55 SWIRL TREE

1.
2.
3.
4. ADD YOUR OWN DECORATIONS!

56 SQUIGGLY TREE

1.
2.
3.
4. ADD SOME TINSEL AND RIBBONS!

THE GOOD AND THE BEAUTIFUL | DRAWING 100 FUN AND EASY TREES

28

57 HEART TREE #2

58 OVAL TREE

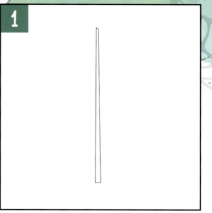
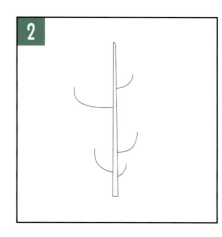
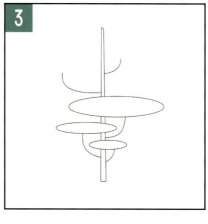
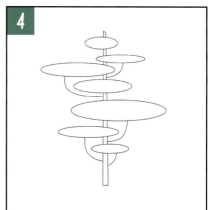

59 BAOBAB TREE

60 TRIANGLE TREE #3

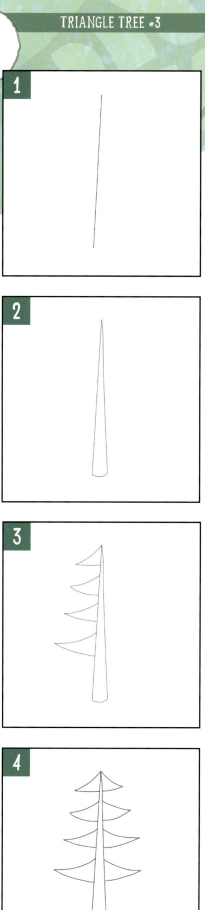

61 FULL TREE

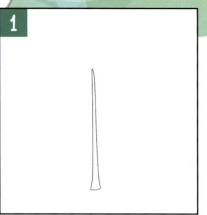
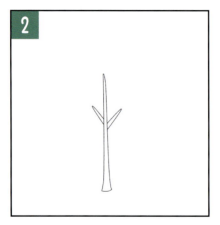

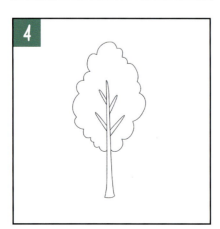

62 LEAFY TREE #2

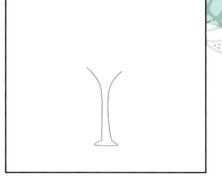
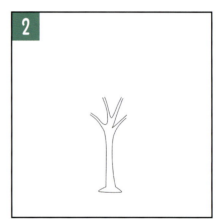
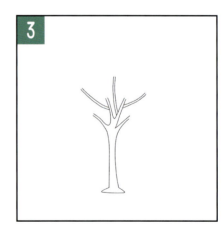
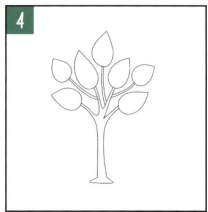

63 EYELASH TREE

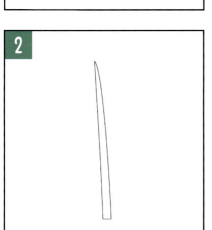
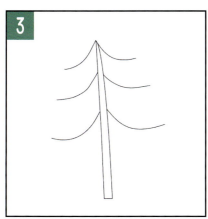
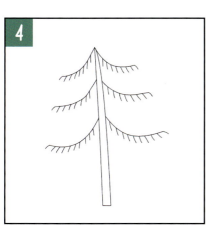

64 CHEVRON TREE #2

65 TREE WITH MANY LEAVES

1

2
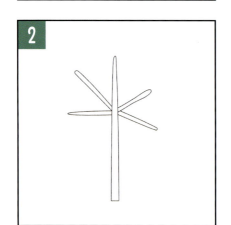

3

4

66 SCALLOPED TREE

1

2

3

4

67 GEOMETRIC TREE

68 STRING TREE

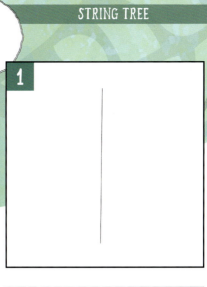

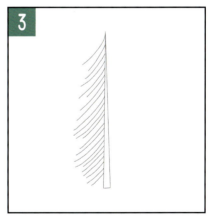

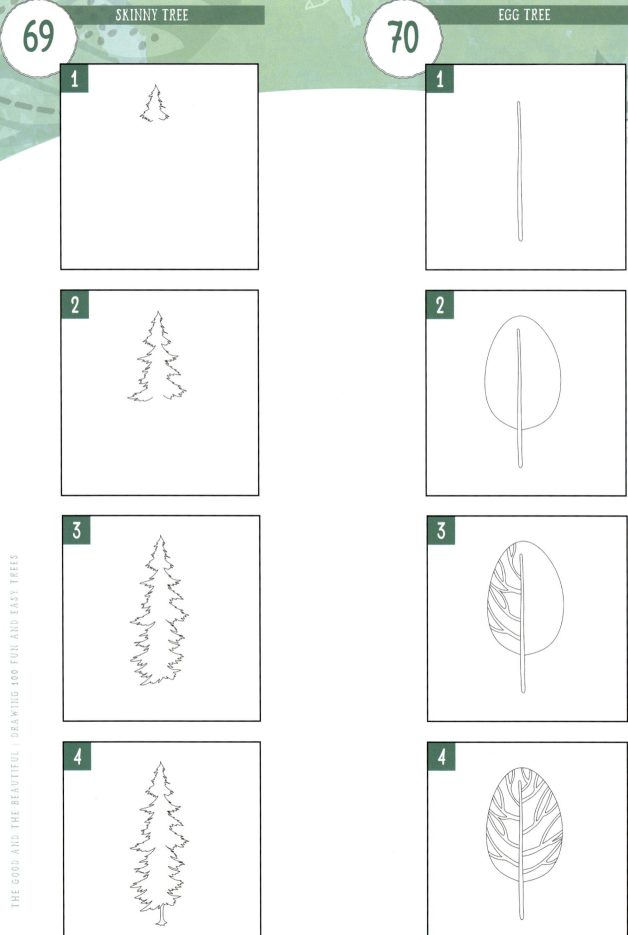

71 BUSHY TREE

1 **2** **3** **4**

72 LARGE TREE

1 **2** **3** **4**

73 BALLOON TREE

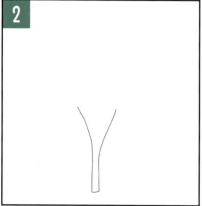

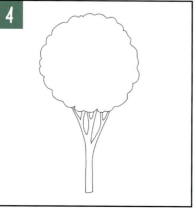

74 SNOWY BRANCHES TREE

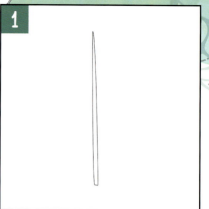

75 — LEAFY BRANCHES ON A TREE

76 — SQUARE TREE

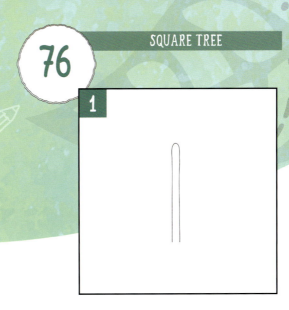

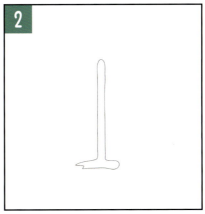

ADD BLOSSOMS TO THE TREE!

77 TWIRLY BUSH TREE

1
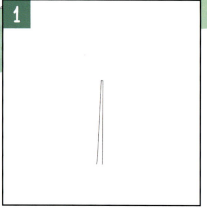

2
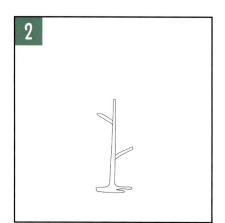

3

4

78 TEARDROP TREE #4

1

2

3

4

79 ROSEBUD TREE

1 **2** **3** **4**

80 POLKA DOT TREE #2

1 **2** **3** **4**

COLOR IN THE POLKA DOTS!

THE GOOD AND THE BEAUTIFUL | DRAWING 100 FUN AND EASY TREES

40

81 — EVERGREEN TREE #5

ADD SOME PINE CONES TO THIS TREE!

82 — ARTSY TREE

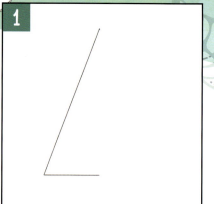
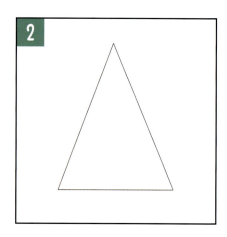
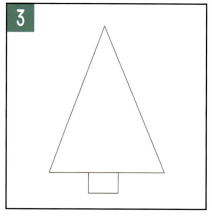

83 TORNADO TREE

84 CURLY TREE #2

85 CONE TREE

86 CURL TREE

87 PETAL TREE

88 WIDE TREE

89 WOODEN BOARD TREE

90 RAINY TREE

91 TALL CONE TREE

92 WILD EVERGREEN TREE

COLOR WITH YOUR FAVORITE COLOR!

ADD A BACKGROUND FOR THIS TREE!

93 TWIGGY TREE

1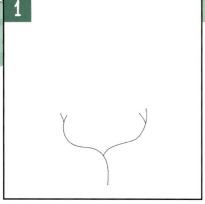

2

3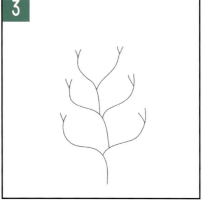

4

94 TALL POINTED TREE

1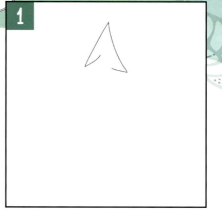

2

3

4

95 BIG ROUND TREE

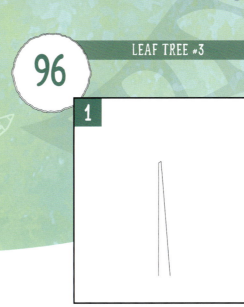

96 LEAF TREE #3

COLOR THIS TREE!

97 CACTUS TREE

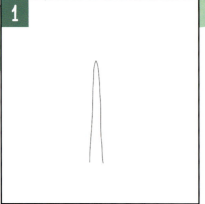
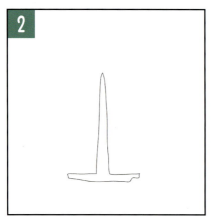

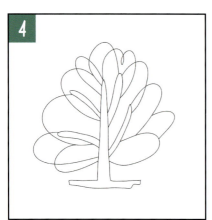

98 TREE WITH BERRIES

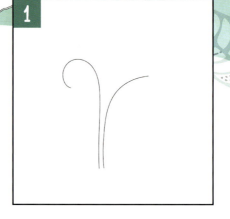

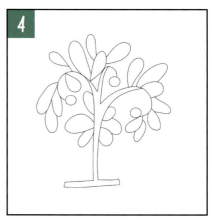

99 — SQUIGGLE TREE WITH A STAR

1

2

3

4
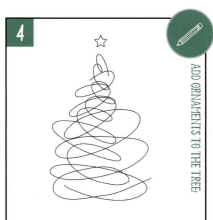

ADD ORNAMENTS TO THE TREE!

100 — FLOURISH TREE

1
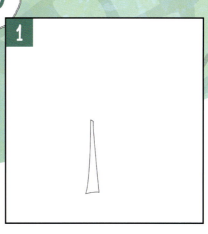

2

3

4
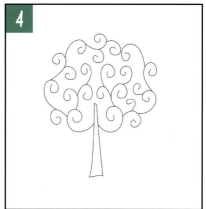

COMPLETE THIS SCENE BY TRACING THESE TREES AND THEN ADDING SOME OF YOUR OWN TREES

HERE ARE SOME ADDITIONAL DRAWING BOOKS FROM THE GOOD AND THE BEAUTIFUL.

DRAW VINTAGE IMAGES

Aspiring artists, young and old, learn through simple steps to draw vintage images like those found in classic storybooks.

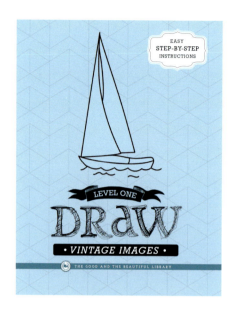
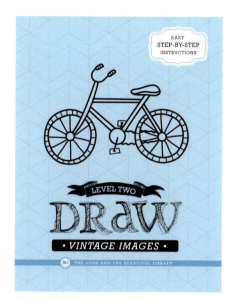

Sample from Level 1

Sample from Level 2

Sample from Level 3

Sample from Level 4

Sample from Level 5

DISCOVER NEW ADVENTURES IN OUR SILVER TALES SERIES.

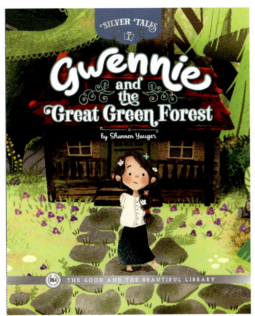

Gwennie and the Great Green Forest
by Shannen Yauger

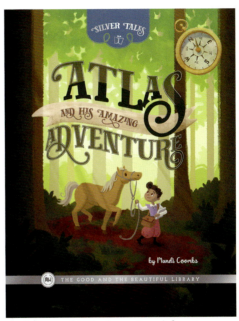

Atlas and His Amazing Adventure
by Mandi Coombs

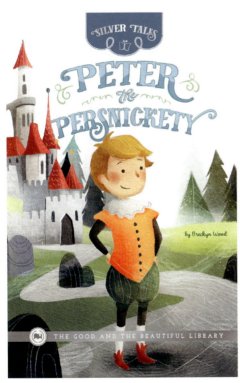

Peter the Persnickety
by Breckyn Wood

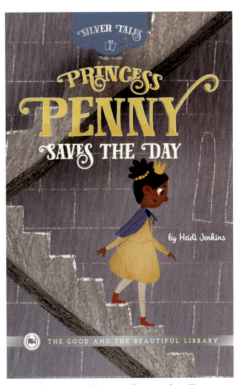

Princess Penny Saves the Day
by Heidi Jenkins

FREE DRAW

FREE DRAW

FREE DRAW